THE NOT-SO-MINOR LEAGUES

THE NOT-SO-MINOR LEAGUES

DOUGLAS GAY AND KATHLYN GAY

The Millbrook Press
Brookfield, Connecticut

Library of Congress Cataloging-in-Publication Data
Gay, Douglas.
The not-so-minor leagues / Douglas Gay and Kathlyn Gay.
p.   cm.
Includes bibliographical references and index.
Summary: The history of the minor leagues, including the major
league success stories of former minor players, how the league
system is organized, and the inner workings of the business of
minor league baseball. Includes information on hometown teams,
collecting autographs, and events sponsored by booster clubs.
ISBN 1-56294-921-7 (lib. bdg.)
1. Minor league baseball—United States—History—Juvenile
literature.   I. Gay, Kathlyn.   II. Title.
GV863.A1G395   1996
796.357´64´0973—dc20   95-43848   CIP   AC

Published by The Millbrook Press
2 Old New Milford Road, Brookfield, Connecticut 06804

To Maggie
Thanks for your belief in me—
not just in the writing of this book
(which I appreciate) but in every other
aspect as well—D.G.

My salute, too,
to this special person—K.G.

Photographs courtesy of Douglas Gay: pp. 15, 19, 20, 26, 29, 37, 55, 88; Robert Aurbach, Albuquerque Dukes: pp. 28, 97; Mark McKenna: p. 45; Eugene Emeralds: p. 48 (top); Toledo Mud Hens: pp. 48 (bottom), 86; Randy LeGrand: p. 60; New Haven Ravens Baseball Club: p. 66; Kathlyn Gay: pp. 57, 68, 75, 79, 89; Calgary Cannons Baseball Club: p. 93; Greg Johnston, Albuquerque Dukes: p. 100. Illustration on p. 40 by Frank Senyk.

CONTENTS

We appreciate the cooperation and help of numerous individuals with minor league ball clubs who provided information and background materials for this book. We cannot name all of them, but we would like to especially thank John Baxter with the South Bend, Indiana, Silver Hawks; Kevin Gilsdorf with the Kane County Cougars in Geneva, Illinois; Rick Rungaitis with the Iowa Cubs in Des Moines; Greg Scharlach with the Rancho Cucamonga (California) Quakes; David O. Sheriff with the Albuquerque (New Mexico) Dukes; Kyle York with the Durham (North Carolina) Bulls; John Olguin with the Los Angeles Dodgers; Joan McGrath with the Arizona Fall League in Phoenix; Mike Hirshfeld with the Ottawa (Canada) Lynx; Marvin Julich with the Winston-Salem (North Carolina) Warthogs; Mary Lee Weber with the New Haven (Connecticut) Ravens; John Traub with the Calgary Cannons in Alberta, Canada; James Konecny with the Toledo (Ohio) Mud Hens; and Bryan Beban with the Eugene (Oregon) Emeralds.

THE
NOT-
SO-
MINOR
LEAGUES

1 FROM BANDITS TO POLECATS!

If you're an ardent baseball fan—or even if you aren't— you probably have heard or read about teams like the Chattanooga Lookouts, Quad City River Bandits, South Bend Silver Hawks, Rancho Cucamonga Quakes, Albany Polecats, or New Haven Ravens. These and other minor league baseball teams have become increasingly popular, drawing more than 32 million spectators in 1995.

Many young people are interested in minor league baseball because they dream of joining a professional team someday. But among young and old nationwide, the groundswell of new and renewed interest in the minor leagues can be traced in part to the popular 1988 movie *Bull Durham*, which was filmed at the Durham Athletic Park in Durham, North Carolina. The movie (starring Kevin Costner, Susan Sarandon, and Tim

Robbins) is a dramatization of life in the minor leagues, and has been called one of the best-ever baseball stories.

Certainly interest in the minor leagues soared when Michael Jordan, once-retired Chicago Bulls basketball superstar, announced in late 1993 that he wanted to try his skills at baseball. During his teenage years, Jordan had played with the Babe Ruth League and then with his high school team at Wilmington Laney High School in North Carolina, but he had never before played professional baseball.

In December, Jordan worked out with a Chicago White Sox trainer at Comiskey Park, and in early 1994 he went to spring training as a non-roster player. He soon signed as a right fielder for the Birmingham (Alabama) Barons. Of course fans came to see him play, and even though his game was hardly spectacular, he was a major attraction and was hounded by the news media. After one game when Jordan met about sixty reporters outside the visitors' clubhouse, police officers had to hold back fans who tried to climb a chain-link fence to get near their hero.

WHAT'S SO SPECIAL ABOUT THE MINORS?

The opportunity to see the world's greatest basketball player attempt a new career in baseball is rare, so obviously there are other factors that draw fans to minor league games. For one, you are able to get closer to the playing field because of reduced seating in minor league parks. Also, total costs for minor league tickets, souvenirs, and refreshments are much lower than they are at

Spectators sit close to the field in a minor league ballpark, so it's easy for fans to get a player's autograph— a favorite activity.

major league baseball games (and the taste of the hot dogs remains basically the same). For example, one of the best seats in County Stadium in Milwaukee, home of the major league Brewers, is almost three times the price of the best seat for a minor league Kane County Cougars game in Geneva, Illinois.

In the Washington, D.C., area, a frequent spectator at Class A Prince William Cannons' games put it this way:

> It's cheap entertainment. For $4 or $5, you can't beat it. I haven't been to Oriole Park [in Baltimore] because it's too far and too expensive... with tickets, parking and food, it costs $128 for four people. Here it costs about $20 for four with a round of cold drinks, and I'm only five or 10 minutes from my house. [1]

Another minor league plus is that fans have an opportunity to see potential major leaguers on their way up as well as current ballplayers who are "doing rehab"—getting back in shape after being injured or disabled in some way. The major leaguer on the mend may need help with mechanical aspects of the game. In the minors, a player

WHADDAYA KNOW...?

Kids have been hitting a ball with some type of stick or bat for as long as recorded history, although in some cases the ball was a walnut wrapped in rags, or some other object.

is able to fine-tune the basics, such as fielding, hitting, and throwing, to get his skills back to major league level.

Consider Ryne Sandberg, who came out of retirement for the 1996 season to again play with the Chicago Cubs. One of the highest-paid players in the game, he received a $5.1 million annual salary in 1993. That year, during the opening game of spring training in Arizona, the Giants' Mike Jackson threw a pitch that hit Sandberg's left hand, breaking it. At first Sandberg reacted with anger and frustration, but later, after surgery that successfully repaired his hand, he pointed out that being injured was "part of the game, an unfortunate happening."

Nevertheless, he had to be out of the game so the hand could mend, and he missed what he called "the fun part of the year"—playing in spring training. By the time his hand had healed, the major league season had started. So Sandberg was sent to Florida, home of two of the Cubs' minor league teams.

Sandberg played two games with the Cubs' Class A Daytona club, and two doubleheaders for AA Orlando, getting batting and fielding opportunities until he was ready to return to Chicago. While with these minor league teams, Sandberg had to adjust to their rules. He was fined twice for uniform dress code violations: once for not showing enough blue on his socks, the other for wearing a gray T-shirt instead of a blue one. He also had to adapt to a different lifestyle. One of the postgame traditions in the majors is a nice spread of food for the players. But when Sandberg asked what the farm team was being served after a game, he was told there were leftover hot dogs at the concession stand.

Obviously, even superstars receive no special privileges. But that didn't faze Sandberg. "It was good for me. It reminded me of what the path is to get [to stardom]," he said. [2]

Sandberg's more humble status did not dampen the enthusiasm of fans. In fact, attendance doubled in both towns when he appeared. People who were seldom able to attend nearby major league games had the opportunity to see an All-Star major league player, nine-time Gold Glove winner, and probable Hall of Famer. Fans, temporary teammates, managers, and ballpark employees were not only able to get a close look at Sandberg, many were also able to get his autograph, a sometimes difficult if not impossible feat at a major league game.

THE MAJOR LEAGUE STRIKE

Increasing attention focused on minor league baseball during the major league baseball strike of 1994 and 1995. Many fans turned to the minors for what they called "pure baseball," without the majors' tension and the bickering about labor issues. Fans frequently said they had been major league fanatics, but after attending minor league games declared their allegiance to the sport in their own backyards. One season-ticket holder for the Firebirds, an affiliate of the San Francisco Giants in Scottsdale, Arizona (a suburb of Phoenix), said, "If there's better baseball than this, I'd like to find it." [3] Attendance increased twofold at Scottsdale Stadium, and the Firebirds chalked up a banner year in 1994.

Some major league fans expressed frustration with owners and players, particularly when the strike wore

While fans stake out viewing spots on the lawn and in the bleachers at the Cougars' stadium in Kane County, Illinois, a player warms up.

on into early 1995. As one disgruntled fan in Goshen, Indiana, pointed out:

The last time I attended a major league game, the tickets were hard to get and expensive, the parking was costly, the hot dogs cost three times what they would anywhere else, the seats were high in the stands, the view was poor, and we left at the end of the sixth inning to avoid the traffic jam. Maybe—just maybe—the time has come to boycott the whole major league business and start all over again. Why not begin with home teams for post-high school players . . . . The ball parks are (for the most part) already in place. Let the fans become involved once again

Pete Rose, Jr., of the Silver Hawks (son of the famous major leaguer) pauses with a young fan during the playing of the National Anthem before the game begins in South Bend, Indiana.

in rooting for the "home team." Let them sing again, "if they don't win, it's a shame," in honest competition and good fun.[4]

The baseball strike also brought frustration and conflict and much media attention to minor league players. Representatives from the players' union warned that if minor leaguers played during spring-training exhibition games, they would be considered strikebreakers. And some major league players threatened minor leaguers with physical harm if they played.

In some instances, team managers made it clear they did not want their young prospects to be subjected to the repercussions of crossing the picket line, but others offered bonuses to minor leaguers who would do exactly that. It was not easy to make a decision. No matter how eager some players were for the opportunity to show off skills, many were leery about going against the union or thought it was unethical to do so. For example, minor league shortstop Gary Green, who was assigned in 1995 to the Kansas City Royals' Triple-A affiliate in Omaha, Nebraska, was asked by several big-league teams to be a replacement player. But Green decided to turn down the offers. During his career he had had three short stints in the big leagues, and, as he put it: "I benefitted from the union. They helped me during the course of my career so I had no desire to be part of [the replacement situation]. If I get back to the big leagues, I want to get back in a normal way."[5]

Nevertheless, some minor leaguers, including those who once played in the majors, felt that playing during spring training was an opportunity to get back to doing something they loved. A *USA Today* survey in early 1995

WHADDAYA KNOW...?

The baseball game played in the United States has its roots in England; the British colonists brought cricket and other stick-and-ball games to North America.

found that of the 125 minor league free agents interviewed, 39 percent said they would definitely or probably sign contracts to replace striking big leaguers. Dennis "Oil Can" Boyd, who signed with the Chicago White Sox, noted that at thirty-five years of age this was likely to be his last opportunity to go to the big leagues. "I'm going to do everything it takes to get there," he told a reporter.

Clubs from all across the United States recruited replacement players, who may or may not have had minor league experience. In Atlanta, for example, approximately 1,300 prospects showed up for tryouts for replacement players for the Braves' spring training games, even though the weather was cold and rainy and no schedule had been set for the training camp. Among the hopefuls were minor leaguers as well as amateur church-league players and even a foursome who played fast-pitch softball and had traveled to Atlanta from Canada. Scouts on hand said they'd never seen such a huge crowd at a tryout.

Once the baseball strike was temporarily resolved in early April 1995, the question of who would or would not be a replacement player was no longer debatable. Some ballclubs paid the promised bonuses to the players who had to return to the minors—$25,000 apiece in the case of the Florida Marlins, which was such a surprise to players that infielder Nick Capra noted: "Guys did cartwheels. I think we had a couple heart attacks. It was awesome." [6]

With the strike over, players and baseball fans turned their attention to the games. However, the games were in the minor leagues. The season opened with the first pitch thrown on April 6 in New Haven, Connecticut, home of the Ravens, affiliate of the Colorado Rockies. Opening games were played in dozens of other cities across the United States while the major league teams were training, and fans in nearly every state, including the less populated ones, such as Idaho and Montana, were anxious to support their favorite minor league teams.

2
HISTORY OF THE MINOR LEAGUES

The minor league system certainly is not new. It's been around almost as long as organized baseball, although in a constant state of flux. Some sports historians say the minor leagues had their start in 1901, when the National Association of Professional Baseball Leagues (NAPBL) was born and independent minor leagues were organized. But others trace the beginnings back to 1877, when three minor league baseball circuits formed under the International Association (IA), the League Alliance (LA), and the New England League.

The IA and LA were associated with and encouraged by the National League, established in 1876 as the first "major" league, but the New England League had no ties with the big-league circuit. A player with any one of the league teams, however, could be picked to play in the major league circuit. Usually the leagues played fewer than twenty games a season, and games were scheduled for weekends because players had to work at their full-time jobs during the rest of the week.

All three of the early minor leagues folded within a few years or operated off and on during the late 1800s. Dozens of other minor leagues quickly formed in the 1880s and 1890s, but many of them were also short-lived. Early minor leagues were often state organizations, such as the Connecticut, Kansas, Ohio State, and Texas Leagues. Regional leagues also formed, including the Central Atlantic League, the Tri-State League in the Midwest, and the Northwestern League with teams from the state of Washington and from British Columbia. A Canadian League established in 1899 included teams primarily from the province of Ontario.

CHANGES IN STRUCTURE

While some minor leagues have come and gone, some have had staying power. The International League, for example, originated in 1884 and has been active ever since, while the Northwest League was active from 1901 to 1922, then again from 1937 to 1942, and from 1946

WHADDAYA KNOW...?

Before baseball became officially known by that name, the game was periodically called stick ball, town ball, goal ball, barn ball, base, and base ball, along with other names.

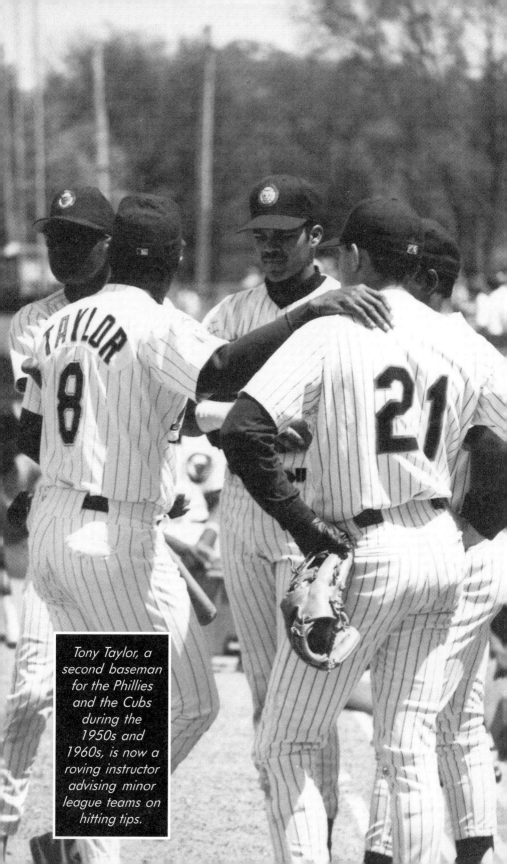

Tony Taylor, a second baseman for the Phillies and the Cubs during the 1950s and 1960s, is now a roving instructor advising minor league teams on hitting tips.

to the present time. Founded in 1901, the American Association operated from 1902 until 1962, when it suspended; teams franchised to play within their circuit moved to the Pacific Coast League or the International League or dropped out of baseball altogether. By 1969, though, the American Association had reactivated and in 1995 included eight Class AAA affiliates.

In the late 1800s and early 1900s, minor leagues were independent of the majors, and competition among major league clubs to obtain players from the minor leagues was intense. A club with the National League or the American League (which declared major league status in 1901) would shamelessly raid the other league's minor teams, and would sometimes sign up players already under contract without compensating the minor league team. Or the major league teams would get into bidding wars to purchase a minor league player's contract. As a result, the minor leagues had to find a way to protect themselves. In 1901 they formed the National Association of Professional Baseball Leagues (NAPBL), which still exists.

The NAPBL, usually called the National Association, established rules for player contracts and allowed major league teams to draft no more than one player per year from any minor league club, increasing to eight per year by 1911. The National Association also set up a classification system for minor leagues that ranged from A at the top to D at the bottom. Over the decades, classifications have changed numerous times, and a graduating system for moving players up through the ranks is an important part of the minor league structure today.

Yet major league teams did not have direct affiliations with minor league teams until 1920, when Branch Rickey developed what is known as the farm system. Rickey, president of the St. Louis Cardinals at the time, could not afford to buy players from independent minor leagues, so he set up a farm club of his own to train and cultivate players.

As this system proved successful, other major league teams also established farm clubs, and by the 1940s all major league teams had developed minor professional teams in which players could work on fundamentals under the guidance of experienced coaches. Today almost all minor league teams that are part of the National Association are affiliated with big-league clubs.

An exciting play, such as a stolen base, is just one of the many attractions that draw fans to both major and minor league baseball games.

Minor league players usually take time out to talk to their admirers.

CHANGES IN PUBLIC INTEREST

Over the years, public interest in minor league ball has had its ups and downs. After World War II, the number of minor leagues peaked at fifty-nine, with more than four hundred franchised teams scattered across the United States. But the number of leagues dwindled steadily to twenty-one by 1959, due particularly to the fact that people could watch major league baseball on television, thus were not as likely to go to minor league ballgames.

In the 1980s, interest in the minor leagues was sparked once more, perhaps because clubs playing within the leagues were operating in a more businesslike manner, using advertising and promotional techniques to help draw crowds. Another factor in the growing popularity has been the increase in the number of minor league teams, brought on in part by the expansion of the National League, which added two clubs, the Colorado Rockies and the Florida Marlins in 1993. The Arizona Diamondbacks and the Tampa Bay Devil Rays are two more recently organized expansion teams expected to play in 1998. There is talk as well of a third major league. In fact, the United Baseball League, founded in 1994 as an independent league, expects to compete with the major leagues in the years ahead as they expand their eight teams in North America with teams in Asia. So more minor league players are needed, adding to hometown interest as fans watch their favorites move up, or switch their allegiance to players who are part of new teams in the minors.

OUTSIDE THE "SYSTEM"

Until about the 1950s, professional baseball in the United States was predominantly a white man's game. Racism, discrimination, and segregation throughout most of U.S. history prevented black ballplayers from being part of organized baseball for many decades. Blacks were forced to form their own baseball teams, and sometimes played and won exhibition games against white teams in the late 1860s.

By the 1870s and 1880s, some black players were allowed to join white teams. The first to make it to the majors was Moses Fleetwood Walker, a catcher for the American Association's Toledo team in 1884. He later played with the Canadian International League. But Walker and other black players in the United States and Canada were subjected to bigoted racist attacks and their lives were often threatened. Increasingly, major league teams refused to play against all-black clubs or any club with black members. By the late 1880s, white clubs would no longer recruit any black ballplayers.

Nevertheless, such leagues as the Negro National League and the Eastern Colored League were formed. They were not part of the organized major league system, but many teams were major league caliber. Black teams ran a regular season, including a World Series, and played in communities across the United States and also in Canada, Japan, and Latin America—primarily in Cuba, Puerto Rico, and Mexico.

Although Negro leagues struggled to survive and players were often subjected to brutality, the teams were showcases for numerous players. Jackie Robinson was playing with the all-black Kansas City Monarchs in 1945 when scouts sent by Branch Rickey, who was president of the Brooklyn Dodgers at the time, noticed him and recommended Robinson for his team. Robinson became the first black player since 1884 to integrate major league baseball. Roy Campanella, Hank Aaron, Willie Mays, and Ernie Banks are just a few others who went from the Negro leagues to organized baseball. All five were elected to the Baseball Hall of Fame in Cooperstown, New York.

With a couple of notable exceptions, women, too, were excluded from organized baseball. However, a few girls and women, such as Alta Weiss of Ragersville, Ohio, pitcher for the Vermilion Independents, were able to join semiprofessional men's teams during the early 1900s. And some young women became part of professional women's teams, playing by special "girls rules" and using a ball larger than the regulation hardball.

When the United States entered World War II in 1941, the major leagues lost most of their players to the draft or voluntary military service. The minor leagues that supplied new talent were also demolished when players were recruited. By the end of 1942, there were fears that major league baseball would have to be canceled for the 1943 season. Although the major league games were played, Philip Wrigley, owner of the Chicago Cubs, had come up with the idea of featuring professional women's teams as a way to maintain public interest in baseball. Women were replacing men in factory jobs and on farms, and the time seemed right to introduce the All-American Girls Professional Baseball League (AAGPBL).

Launched in 1943, the AAGPBL comprised four teams: the Racine Belles and Kenosha Comets in Wisconsin, the Blue Sox in South Bend, Indiana, and the Peaches in Rockford, Illinois. These and other early women's leagues played softball at first, but soon showed they could play regular hardball.

WHADDAYA KNOW...?

Players used no gloves in early baseball games, and pitchers threw the ball underhanded.

The league expanded after the war, adding the Grand Rapids (Michigan) Chicks and the Fort Wayne (Indiana) Daisies in 1945, and the Muskegon (Michigan) Lassies and the Peoria (Illinois) Redwings in 1946. Other teams formed during the late 1940s and early 1950s, and there were plans for a minor league system to prepare girls for the AAGPBL.

Even though the skills and quality of the games in women's baseball often approximated that of players in the male-dominated major leagues, attendance at AAGPBL games began to decline. Several factors played a role. Americans had become more mobile and were no longer dependent on hometown entertainment. Or they were caught up in the new age of television. In addition, there was a strong social movement to encourage women to leave public life and go back to "their place" in the home. Finally, poor management of the AAGPBL forced the organization to disband in 1954.

Girls and women continued to play softball and baseball over the years, but they were not officially recognized again as professional players until the early 1990s. Today the main emphasis for women is softball, particularly at the college level. One notable exception is the Colorado Silver Bullets, an all-women's team owned by Whittle Communications and Coors Brewing Company. Inspired by the movie *A League of Their Own* about the AAGPBL, the Class A team was formed in 1994 and is managed by former Atlanta Braves' pitcher Phil Niekro.

Reportedly, each of the twenty women signed up for the Silver Bullets earns $20,000 annually, compared with $3,000 per year earned by a player in a single-A independent league. During the 1994 season, the Silver Bullets competed in exhibition games against semipro and independent all-male teams.

3 TODAY'S MINOR LEAGUES

If you've never been to a minor league game, you might wonder what to expect when you go to a community park for the first time. You're likely to notice that the infield dimensions are the same as those of the major leagues—distance from the pitching rubber to home plate is 60 feet, 6 inches, and the basepaths are 90 feet long. Outfield dimensions vary (although there are minimum requirements for outfield distances), but they are similar to those of major league parks, particularly the ones built in urban areas and surrounded by factories, stores, shops, apartment buildings, and homes.

There are some differences in the look and atmosphere of minor league parks compared to the majors. More billboard advertising covers outfield walls and fences in minor league parks. There are fewer seats in the minors—most parks have between 5,000 and 10,000 seats, while there are 35,000 to 65,000 seats in the majors. Also, recently built minor league stadiums typically have theater-style single seats with arm rests, arranged so that customers have an unobstructed view of the field no matter where they sit. Seats are much closer to the playing field as well.

In many ways, going to a minor league park is like attending a community gathering. Many parks include grassy areas for picnicking or roomy parking lots where fans can tailgate—serve food and drinks from the back of a station wagon, van, or truck. A special drive-in parking area in Albuquerque allows fans to not only tailgate

YALE FIELD

It was once an apple orchard, and in 1865 became the home of Yale University's varsity baseball squad. Today, Yale Field is a state-of-the-art modern ballpark where the minor league New Haven Ravens play. But long-time fans and newcomers alike are often reminded of the park's illustrious past during which presidents have watched games and some of America's baseball greats have performed. According to an account written by Danny Goldman for the New Haven Ravens' 1995 Game Program, one of the most dramatic moments on the field occurred in 1948 when Babe Ruth appeared for the last time. He was suffering from cancer and near death. But Ruth walked slowly to the infield and presented Yale captain George Bush (yes, former president George Bush) with a donation to the university library—an original manuscript of Ruth's autobiography.

A grounds-
keeper rakes
and grooms
the baseline
before a
minor league
game begins.

WHADDAYA KNOW...?

Ladies' Day—allowing women free admittance to the ballpark—was introduced to professional baseball in 1887 by a New Orleans minor league player and manager, Charles Abner Powell. Powell is credited also with introducing the rain check, which admitted fans to another game if the current one was postponed.

but also watch the game from their vehicles. Even new urban parks, such as the stadium in downtown Durham, North Carolina, feature picnic areas.

But what about the teams themselves? Who are they? Where and when do they play? How are they organized? Who owns them?

THE MINOR LEAGUE TEAMS

Minor league teams are professional teams just as the majors are. That is, players are paid for what they do, but they earn much less than those who've signed contracts with the majors. Their status depends on their team's classification, which ranges from AAA (next thing to The Show—the majors), AA, A, Short-Season Class A, and Rookie Short Season.

The major league clubs usually have working agreements with teams in all the classifications. In 1995, for example, affiliates of the San Diego Padres were the Las Vegas Stars (AAA) in Las Vegas, Nevada; Memphis Chicks (AA) in Memphis, Tennessee; Rancho Cucamonga Quakes (A) in Rancho Cucamonga, California; Clinton Lumber Kings (A) in Clinton, Iowa; Idaho Falls Padres (Short Season A) in Idaho Falls, Idaho; and the Peoria Padres (Rookie Short Season) in Peoria, Arizona.

Classified teams compete within leagues organized geographically across North America. The top AAA leagues are the American Association, International, and Pacific Coast. Another Triple-A league is the Mexican League, but it is basically a separate entity and provides opportunities primarily for Mexican players. Teams that make up the Eastern, Southern, and Texas Leagues are in the AA classification. And the California, Carolina, Florida State, Midwest, and South Atlantic Leagues are made up of Class A teams.

Each of the leagues may consist of anywhere from just a few teams to more than a dozen. The number of teams changes frequently, although the Class A South Atlantic League of fourteen teams has been fairly stable in recent times. In 1995 it included the Albany (Georgia) Polecats affiliated with the Montreal Expos of Canada; the Augusta (Georgia) Greenjackets with the Pittsburgh Pirates; the Charleston, West Virginia, Alley Cats with the Cincinnati Reds; and the Piedmont Phillies in Kannapolis, North Carolina, with the Philadelphia Phillies.

The Triple-A Pacific Coast League includes the Calgary Cannons and Edmonton Trappers in Alberta, Canada, and the Vancouver Canadians in Vancouver, British Columbia. Other teams are in Albuquerque, New

PACIFIC COAST LEAGUE , TRIPLE A

Mexico; Colorado Springs, Colorado; Las Vegas, Nevada; Salt Lake City, Utah; Tacoma, Washington; and Tucson, Arizona.

The number of games the leagues play varies. Rookie ball is an abbreviated season of seventy-two games—thirty-six home games, thirty-six away. For AAA, AA, and A ball, the season is 142 games compared with the traditional 162 for the majors, although there were fewer major league games in the 1994 and 1995 seasons because of the strike.

Why do the minors have shorter seasons than the majors? When the season is over for the minors in September, the major league clubs expand their rosters (from twenty-five to forty players). That way they can bring in young players to check out their skills. Managers and coaches evaluate, for example, whether a minor league pitcher can pitch to major league hitters or whether a batter can hit major league pitching. The big club can decide whether to invest more time and money in a player or keep him in the minors.

INDEPENDENT TEAMS AND LEAGUES

Although the vast majority of minor league teams are affiliates of major league clubs, some independent minor league teams operate without working agreements with majors. In 1994 one such team was the Class A San Bernardino Spirit in San Bernardino, California. Spirit owners were responsible for all operating expenses of the club, players' salaries, uniforms, and travel—in short, everything it takes to run a ballclub. But the costs

WHADDAYA KNOW...?

In 1858 a field owner in Long Island charged admission for the first time—it cost fifty cents to see a game.

of maintaining the team and getting a high level of talent became prohibitive. As a result, the team was sold to the Los Angeles Dodgers organization in 1995 and became a Class A affiliate of the Dodgers.

There are also a few independent leagues, which are outside organized baseball; they are associated with neither the big clubs nor the National Association. One is the Northern League, made up of six teams—two of them in Canada. Another is the Mid-America League, inaugurated in the spring of 1995 with a sixty-game schedule. It includes four Indiana teams with home bases in the cities of Merrillville, East Chicago, Anderson, and Lafayette.

The Class AA Texas-Louisiana League is also independent, but varies from most in that all its teams are owned by one person—Carl Westcott, a Texas millionaire. At the end of the 1994 season, the Abilene (Texas) Prairie Dogs became part of this league, providing Abilene with its first professional team since 1957. Two more teams were added to the league during the winter of 1994–1995.

In April 1995 the Atlantic League of Professional Baseball was formed. An independent league in the Northeast, it will include six teams, scheduled to begin play in 1997. Homes of the teams are Atlantic City and Newark in New Jersey; Charlottesville, Virginia; Lehigh Valley, Pennsylvania; Long Island, New York; and Lowell, Massachusetts.

IN THE SYSTEM

Among the more than five thousand minor league players in North America, only an estimated 5 percent will be promoted to the majors. Some players spend all of their professional careers within the minor league system, never making it to the top. Nevertheless, as Pulitzer Prize-winning political columnist and avid baseball fan George Will explained, "in baseball . . . those who could never do it with major league proficiency, no matter how hard they tried, often are the ones who can teach it well." [1] They may become excellent coaches or managers.

In most instances, when a player nears or passes the age of thirty and hasn't gone on to the big leagues, he may begin considering another career. But it's not uncommon for some to pursue their dream for as long as they can. They keep hoping some top club will show interest in their playing talent.

But talent doesn't always win out. In some cases, a manager or scout dislikes a player and won't do anything to encourage him. A big-league club might have a surplus of, say, outfielders and have no need to bring up a player in that position. Or in a few instances a player's contract is sold to another minor league team that does little to promote his career and, in effect, buries him.

Nevertheless, minor league players can move along in a slow, methodical way, often taking five to seven years to develop before they eventually get a chance at the big time. Still others who are top prospects are catapulted to the majors.

SCOUTING

The process of moving into the majors begins with scouts—all major teams have scouts assigned to certain territories and levels of ball. Some scouts check out prospects in the Arizona Fall League (AFL) established in 1992 by major league baseball and Safeway supermarkets. Only recently has there been much nationwide publicity about the league. As the name implies, it's a fall league and does not compete with winter baseball in Venezuela, Puerto Rico, the Dominican Republic, and Mexico. It has been described as a jumping-off point, a kind of finishing school for players on their way to the big show.

As Mike Port, president of the AFL, explained: "It used to be that most players had 1,000 at-bats or 500 innings pitched before getting to the big leagues, but now players are often rushed to the majors without much experience. With instructional leagues using more and more of the younger players (Class A and Rookie Leagues), baseball finds itself needing more winter jobs."[2]

Teams in the AFL are made up of top major league prospects who need to fine-tune their skills with high-level coaching and instruction. Some need experience against tougher competition than is possible in other

Shawn Holman (#39) and Curtis Pride (#27) of the Ottawa Lynx observe youngsters practicing their skills at the Junior Lynx Baseball Clinic.

leagues. And there are also prospects who may be near the end of their playing days but have a final chance to revive their careers. In short, the AFL has some of the highest levels of talent. Since the league was established, more than one hundred players have gone on to the majors, including Mike Piazza of the Los Angeles Dodgers, Bob Hamelin of the Kansas City Royals, John Hudek of the Houston Astros, and Ryan Klesko of the Atlanta Braves.

How do scouts evaluate players? According to R. J. Harrison, who scouts for the New York Mets and focuses on the AFL in September and October, "some things are obvious: It doesn't take a genius to see that a pitcher throws hard or that a third baseman has a strong arm or that an outfielder has great speed. But as a scout

I must look for some things that are less apparent to the average fan." Harrison finds out whether a player has ever been injured, how long he's been a professional player, how many teams he's played for and at what levels. A player's work ethic, "the amount of effort a player puts forth during pre-game workouts tells me a lot about him," Harrison noted.

Although a radar gun can check the speed of a pitch and a stopwatch can mark foot speed, Harrison depends on his "eyes and experience" to tell him about the sharpness of the break in a curveball or whether a player makes effective use of all of the tools he has, from fielding ability to hitting power. All of the information Harrison gathers on a player is compiled on a scouting card and his report is input on a computer where it can be compared to evaluations by other scouts. In the end, though, "scouting is not an exact science," as Harrison put it, and he, like his counterparts, uses as many tools as possible to size up a player.[3]

Numerous scouts travel around the country checking out college teams. College baseball has played an especially important role in providing talent for professional teams, and there has long been talk of replacing the minor league structure with a recruitment system that depends on college teams, similar to the way players are recruited for professional football and basketball. To date, however, the farm system remains firmly in place.

Just out of college, a player could go to A or AA ball, depending on his talent. The odds for advancement are good, because he has had more playing time at a higher level than a player with only high school or per-

WHADDAYA KNOW...?

In 1869, the first professional baseball team, the Cincinnati Red Stockings, played around the United States, and during the season the team went un-defeated.

haps American Legion team experience. It's not out of the question to go directly from a college team to AAA ball, although it's not too common.

On occasion, a dozen scouts may descend on a town, because they have heard or read about a particular high school player through local news media. If a player is recruited just out of high school, chances are he will go to Rookie ball in, for example, the Appalachian League or the Pioneer League. Rookies play a shorter season (from mid-June to late August), which allows a teen-ager to become acclimated to being away from home, perhaps becoming more disciplined, abiding by curfews, and so on. The short season also allows players to continue their education.

Some high school players become "bonus babies" like Brien Taylor. From a poor family in North River, just outside Beaufort, North Carolina, Taylor has played baseball since he was four years old, developing a power-ful left arm. "By the time I played Little League, I was striking out 15 or 16 batters a game," he nonchalantly told a reporter.[4] Before his thirteenth birthday, he was throwing the ball at 80 miles per hour (129 kph) and at fifteen years old was pitching a fastball clocked at over 90 miles per hour (145 kph).

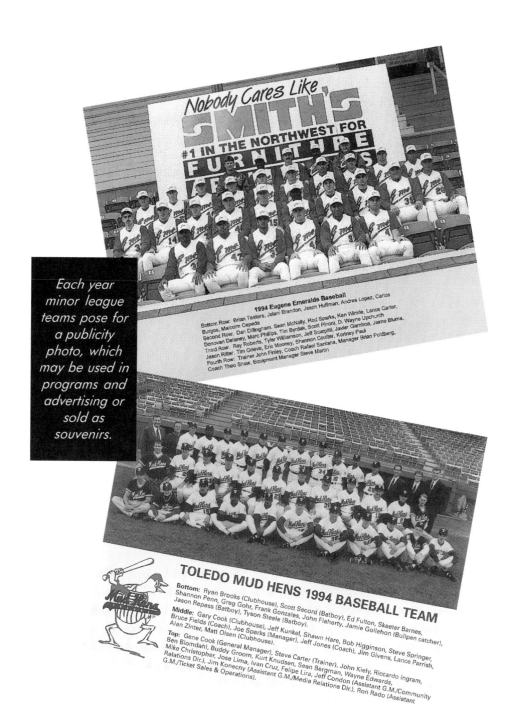

Each year minor league teams pose for a publicity photo, which may be used in programs and advertising or sold as souvenirs.

1994 Eugene Emeralds Baseball
Bottom Row: Brian Teeters, Jelani Brandon, Jason Huffman, Andres Lopez, Carlos Burgos, Malcolm Cepeda
Second Row: Dan Dillingham, Sean McNally, Rod Sparks, Ken Winide, Lance Carter, Donovan Delaney, Marc Phillips, Tim Byrdak, Scott Pinoni, D. Wayne Upchurch
Third Row: Ray Roberts, Tyler Williamson, Jeff Scarpitti, Javier Gamboa, Jaime Bluma, Jason Ritter, Tim Greve, Eric Mooney, Shannon Coulter, Kortney Paul
Fourth Row: Trainer John Finley, Coach Rafael Santana, Manager Brian Poldberg, Coach Theo Shaw, Equipment Manager Steve Martin

TOLEDO MUD HENS 1994 BASEBALL TEAM
Bottom: Ryan Brooks (Clubhouse), Scott Secord (Batboy), Ed Fulton, Skeeter Barnes, Shannon Penn, Greg Gohr, Frank Gonzales, John Flaherty, Jamie Gollehon (Bullpen catcher), Jason Repass (Batboy), Tyson Steele (Batboy).
Middle: Gary Cook (Clubhouse), Jeff Kunkel, Shawn Hare, Bob Higginson, Steve Springer, Bruce Fields (Coach), Joe Sparks (Manager), Jeff Jones (Coach), Jim Givens, Lance Parrish, Alan Zinter, Matt Olsen (Clubhouse).
Top: Gene Cook (General Manager), Steve Carter (Trainer), John Kiely, Riccardo Ingram, Ben Blomdahl, Buddy Groom, Kurt Knudsen, Sean Bergman, Wayne Edwards, Mike Christopher, Jose Lima, Ivan Cruz, Felipe Lira, Jeff Condon (Assistant G.M./Community Relations Dir.), Jim Konecny (Assistant G.M./Media Relations Dir.), Ron Rado (Assistant G.M./Ticket Sales & Operations).

In 1991, his senior year at East Carteret High School in North Carolina, Taylor pitched back-to-back no hitters, which sent scouts scurrying to sign him up. When a New York Yankees scout offered him a bonus of several hundred thousand dollars to join the organization, Brien's mother, who worked for meager wages shucking oysters, stepped in, letting the scout know that her son was worth a lot more. Finally, in 1992, the Yankees offered Brien a record-high bonus of $1.55 million to play Class A ball with their Fort Lauderdale team. Reportedly, Taylor used a portion of the money to build a house for his parents on land where their trailer once stood and paved the dirt road leading to their new home.

But in December 1993, Taylor got into a bar fight trying to defend his brother and injured his left shoulder. He underwent major reconstructive surgery and was out of the game throughout 1994. Doctors predicted he would not throw a baseball again until 1995, but halfway through the 1994 season he began rehabilitation at the Yankees' minor league complex in Tampa, Florida. Although his career is uncertain at this point, Taylor and Yankee officials hope he'll be able to perform as he once did and eventually throw his fastball at Yankee Stadium at 97 to 98 miles per hour (156 to 158 kph).

GOING FULL CIRCLE

Some players move up for a season or two, then return to the minors because they have not played the quality of ball expected. For many, the demotion can be hard to take, a comedown to live and work with inexperienced rookies again. Some may get completely fed up with baseball and quit. Others hang in because they have confidence in their talent and love the game.

A case in point is left-handed pitcher Sherman Corbett, who began playing professional baseball in 1984. He was promoted to the majors in 1988 and appeared with the California Angels for forty-two games over the next three seasons. But in 1990 he was released to play with farm teams affiliated with the Detroit Tigers, then the Chicago Cubs. While with the Class AA Orlando Cubs in 1993, Corbett pointed out that he had other options beside baseball for earning a living, but he enjoyed the game. "It's exciting coming to the park every day to put on the uniform. When it's not fun anymore, I'll give it up," he told a reporter. [5]

Another pitcher, Steve Fireovid of Bryan, Ohio, signed his first professional contract in 1978 and had a taste of the major leagues for parts of six seasons, but spent most of his career in the minors. In a book that chronicles one year (1990) in the minors, Fireovid pointed out, "There are a lot of us, experienced guys stuck at Triple-A as insurance policies, hired to display good work habits to the bonus babies . . . . A lot of us . . . are being groomed as coaches." [6]

In some instances, players with seesaw careers go back to farm teams as coaches or managers and then become successful with the majors in one of those capacities. Such was the case for Tom Lasorda, who pitched for the Brooklyn Dodgers and also the Kansas City Athletics during the 1950s. But he was not destined for stardom as a pitcher. So he became a minor league manager—a highly successful one. Then, in the 1970s, he was hired for the coaching staff of the Dodgers. He was named the Dodgers' manager in 1976. Since then he has spurred his team to six league championship series appearances and four World Series appearances, winning the World Series in 1981 and 1988. Much of the team's success has been attributed to Lasorda's ability to teach players to have fun with the game. He is also actively involved with his team and still works with players during batting practice, which is usually a coach's job. In 1995 he began his nineteenth full year as Dodgers' manager and his forty-sixth with the organization, winning the western division title.

Players who have had long careers in the majors often start a second career in the minors. Rick Dempsey is an example. After a twenty-four-year career as a catcher with six different major league clubs, he took over as manager of the Albuquerque Dukes, a Triple-A Dodger team.

Another example is Jim Colborn. Although his career was not as long as Dempsey's, Colborn pitched for ten years in the majors, then became a roving instructor for the Chicago Cubs. Among the pitchers that he coached was the Atlanta Braves' Greg Maddux, a four-time winner of the Cy Young award in the same number of years (1992-1995). After spending four years in Japan as a coach for one of the Japanese major league teams, Colborn was hired in 1994 as manager of the West Michigan Whitecaps of Grand Rapids, Michigan, the Oakland Athletics' Class A team.

Minor league management and coaching—like playing—hardly bring the monetary rewards possible in the major leagues. But players who return to the minors as coaches or managers often say they have baseball in their blood. Besides that, they can relate well with players because they've been there. And being "there" rather than in the majors is not a different ballgame but certainly a different lifestyle.

4 FROM "BUS LEAGUES" TO THE MAJORS

During Michael Jordan's brief time with the Class AA Birmingham Barons, he rarely complained about the lack of first-class treatment that had long been part of his lifestyle. But he did criticize the mode of transportation for minor league players. While long-distance travel for the majors and some Class AAA ballplayers is usually via chartered planes, lower classification farm teams travel the least expensive way—by bus. In years past, buses were not well maintained and flat tires or engine troubles occurred, although that is not necessarily the case today. However, a long trip by bus can be uncomfortable.

Jordan thought the bus used by the Barons ought to have more leg room. So he bought one himself, replacing the old vehicle with a new $350,000 luxury model—the type used by rock stars on tour. Not only does it have thirty-five reclining seats, it's also equipped with six TV sets, a VCR, and a lounge area with a wet bar.

LIFE "DOWN ON THE FARM"

Few teams are lucky enough to have a benefactor such as Jordan, and frugality is the general rule "down on the farm." In the first place, players who sign up for a Class A club are not likely to earn much more than $1,000 per month, plus about $15 per day meal expenses.

In the independent leagues, such as the Mid-America League, players earn much less. For a team like the Merrillville (Indiana) Muddogs, players were offered a monthly salary of $500 to $700 for the 1995 season—hardly a big financial incentive. But up to 500 potential players, primarily young men who'd been on college teams, tried out, not because of the money but because they might have a chance to play baseball for at least one more season—and get paid for it. Most important was the possibility they would be seen by professional scouts.

Once major league scouts have recorded information about players and prospects have been signed up, players go through spring training at Arizona or Florida baseball complexes. There players are evaluated and then assigned to a classification and a team within the organization.

Rookies going into a strange town or state usually feel pressure both on and off the field. If they have never been out on their own, they may find day-to-day living a struggle. For many, this is the first time they have had

Before fans fill seats in any ballpark, players are out on the field getting batting practice or warming up for the game.

to pay expenses for rent, utilities, and food. They have to learn how to shop and cook, do laundry, and adjust to living with other people and rooming with a teammate while on the road.

When a "bus league" team travels, members usually stay in modest hotels—there are no luxuries. This is not just a cost-saving measure. There is also a motivational factor, some managers say. They don't want players to get too comfortable and to deliberately make a career of the minor league. They want to promote players and get them into the majors. After all, that's the reason minor league farm teams exist.

During the early 1900s, a minor league player named Ten Million (his real name) left baseball and became a Ford car dealer. There was a huge promotion when the 10 millionth Ford rolled off the assembly line.

Even though a town or city strongly supports its home team, players may never really become part of the community. In the words of one rookie who had graduated from an Arlington, Texas, high school and signed with the Southern Oregon Athletics in 1994: "This is my first time away from home . . . . I was nervous the first week or so, but not since then . . . I get homesick some. I call home about three times a week, and they call here quite a bit. And there's a girl I call some."[1]

Some rookies give in to homesickness or other emotional stress and quit. Others manage to deal with whatever emotional traumas there might be, because they know they have a chance to make it to the big leagues. That's been their dream and hope for years, so they focus on the goal.

MAKING IT

Quick promotion through the ranks is not common in the minors, but some players move up at a fairly fast pace—even with setbacks. Consider Scott Radinsky of Simi Valley, California. While in high school he played drums with a band. But he could also play baseball, and in 1986 he was signed by the Chicago White Sox as a pitcher and assigned to their Class A Rookie League team in Sarasota, Florida. Radinsky was out of the game for the 1988 season because of shoulder surgery, but during the winter he continued to play rock music with a quintet he'd formed (and recorded a few minor hits, one titled "Born to Be Wild").

The next year Radinsky was assigned to the Class A South Bend (Indiana) White Sox of the Midwest League. He drove to South Bend from his home in southern California in his VW van, which had a hole in the roof. He had to borrow a tarp to keep rain out of his vehicle.

Players with the Eugene Emeralds Baseball Club meet young autograph seekers at Civic Stadium in Eugene, Oregon.

In South Bend, Radinsky—like others on the team—lived in a low-cost housing complex, sharing an apartment with other players. While the team was at home during the season, Radinsky's daily routine varied little. During the week, he made the trip to the stadium in the middle of town and took part in drills—stretching exercises, lifting weights, and so on. Radinsky was usually the first one on the field, arriving even before the office employees and working out two to four hours before game time. He became the top relief pitcher for the South Bend team, which won the 1989 Midwest League championship.

By the 1990 season, Radinsky was a regular relief pitcher for the Chicago White Sox and stayed with the team through the 1993 season, appearing in 270 games. In 1994 he was again forced out of the game and had to return to California for treatment of Hodgkin's disease, a form of cancer. Fortunately, chemotherapy and radiation were successful.

During the 1994 season, Radinsky kept himself busy by continuing to play with a musical group called the Ten Foot Pole and volunteering as a baseball coach for Simi Valley High School. Twice he threw on the sidelines for the Sox pitching coaches. He told a Chicago Tribune reporter that it was hard to watch Sox games on TV and go out to the park in Anaheim, California, to see his teammates play. The worst part was "not being able to suit up." [2]

In 1995, after the baseball strike was settled, Radinsky rode his motorcycle cross-country to return to the White Sox spring training complex in Florida.

Then it was on to Comiskey Park in Chicago for his turn on the mound once more.

Many players who become professionals just out of high school go on to long careers in the majors. One example is Charlie Hough, called the "ageless knuckleballer," who was drafted by the Dodgers in 1966 out of a Hialeah, Florida, high school. He spent several seasons with the Albuquerque Dodgers, then in 1970 was promoted to the Dodgers' Class AAA club in Spokane, Washington. By 1972 he was a relief pitcher with the Albuquerque Dukes, which had become a Triple-A club. Within a year almost the entire ballclub had gone on to the major leagues. Hough, who pitched part of the 1970, 1971, and 1972 seasons in the majors, became a full-time major league pitcher in 1973 and a starter in 1982 with the Texas Rangers.

After playing with the Chicago White Sox, Hough joined the Florida Marlins in 1993, which brought him back to his home state and close to his hometown. Hough underwent hip replacement surgery after the 1994 season and retired at the age of forty-six, ending a twenty-nine-year career in baseball, all but four of those years

WHADDAYA KNOW...?

Since the 1970s, aluminum bats have been used extensively by amateur baseball teams, from Little League to college ball. They have been considered by minor league teams, but so far have not been adopted or permitted by professionals.

Baseball is a family game with the Boones. Pictured here is third baseman Aaron Boone of the Winston-Salem Warthogs. He is the grandson of former major leaguer Ray Boone, the son of Kansas City Royals manager Bob Boone, and brother of major leaguer Bret Boone of the Cincinnati Reds.

in the big leagues. When the 1995 season opened, Hough was honored with a commemorative pin by the Marlins, but in characteristic fashion shrugged it off as just one of those gimmicks that clubs use to attract fans.

PERSONALITIES OF THE GAME

Seldom are minor league players highly publicized unless they are hot prospects for the major leagues. But some gain reputations and nicknames because of their idiosyncrasies and quirks.

Over the years baseball players have exhibited enough oddities to fill the pages of numerous books. Infielder Mike Maksudian enjoys eating insects and has tattoos of the names of all the teams he's played for—minor and major league. One former minor league third baseman, Drake Hogestyn, once with the Fort Lauderdale Yankees, switched careers after winning a talent contest and became a soap opera star on *Days of Our Lives.*

SHOELESS JOE

In the early 1900s one of the greatest hitters, Joe Jackson, was called "Shoeless Joe" because once, in the minors, he played in his stocking feet; he couldn't tolerate his tight new shoes. Jackson also used a hickory bat that he darkened with tobacco juice, spitting and rubbing it into the wood over and over again.

Frankie Rodriguez, a starting pitcher with the Pawtucket Red Sox of the International League, shaved his head during the 1994 season on a bet with teammates. Then, when he got "in a groove" and was "getting the hitters" he decided to keep his Mr. Clean look. Another minor leaguer, John Massarelli, an outfielder/catcher with the Charlotte Knights, has a hobby that he shares with his young daughter: he likes to fill in coloring books and watch *Barney* on TV.

A great number of baseball players follow superstitious rituals before and during games, although few will admit to such practices. Baseball has frequently been called the most superstitious sport, so it was not surprising to see some "magic" routines dramatized in the movie *Bull Durham,* such as a pitcher wearing women's garters to bring him good luck and players crossing chicken bones to take the curse off a bat. There's plenty of evidence that, in order to bring good luck to the game, players wear certain clothing—a special T-shirt, dirty socks, or a sweat-stained baseball cap under a protective helmet are just a few examples. Ballplayers have also tried to "charm" their bats and gloves with any number of different items, from polished stones to rabbit feet.

WHADDAYA KNOW...?

The official ball used in baseball games weighs 5 ounces (141.75 grams). It is made of cork wound with woolen yarn and covered with two layers of cowhide stitched together by hand.

Other common superstitious practices include eating a specific meal—biscuits and gravy or a chicken dinner—as part of a routine before a game. Some players feel jinxed if they don't travel a specific route to the ballpark. Still others wouldn't think about going up to bat without first spitting on the plate or the dirt beside it.

Individual players frequently have their pet superstitious practices. In 1993 the Orlando Cubs' center fielder Phil Dauphin began a hitting streak. In order to avoid a jinx, he decided to let his hair grow. When the streak ended after nineteen games, he announced that he planned to get a haircut. With the Florida heat, he was getting uncomfortable, he said, and besides his good luck had vanished for the moment.

Pitcher Turk Wendell, who played for brief periods with the Chicago Cubs from 1993 to 1995, has been known for his eccentric behavior on the field, although he's cut back on some antics. It was once common for him to darken the inside bill of his hat with a black marker, and he refused to wear athletic socks because he claimed they caused blisters. He made it a habit to jump over the foul line when going to the dugout, a common practice in baseball to ward off bad luck. He also marked the mound with three Xs and waved to the outfield before he began to pitch. When he was with the Durham Bulls, he used a lead ball for warmups.

One of Wendell's most publicized traits was his big wad of licorice, which he chewed instead of tobacco. He spit out the licorice after coming to the mound, and between each inning he brushed his teeth to get rid of the sugary residue of the candy. But then he stuck another hunk of licorice in his jaw! He started the practice while with the Double-A Greenville, South Carolina, team and told a *Sports Illustrated* reporter that the licorice chaw made him "look more intimidating." Even though his teammates told him he was "a lunatic," he said he didn't care because the chaw gave him "a psychological edge."

5 THE BUSINESS SIDE OF THE GAMES

"Buy Your Own Ball Club," advised a headline a few years ago in the business magazine *Fortune*. It's common knowledge that buying a major league baseball team is a huge investment, but what about buying minor leagues? Can anybody buy a team? That might have been possible in the 1980s when paying off a team's debts was one way to become a team owner. But as the minor leagues have gained popularity, the value of teams has gone up, too.

A Rookie club could sell for a few hundred thousand dollars with the price tag increasing for Class A teams. The Pittsfield (Massachusetts) Mets of the New York–Penn League sold for $850,000 in 1992. But a Triple-A team costs millions. In 1991 the Ottawa Lynx, a Triple-A affiliate of the Montreal Expos, was purchased for $6.4 million.

Today, a top-ranked AAA team would sell for $8–10 million. Obviously the vast majority of Americans don't have access to those kind of funds, although a few investors have purchased limited partnerships, buying a percentage of a team.

Anyone who buys a franchise has to meet specific requirements of the team's major league affiliate, such as following strict standards for locker-room facilities, for example. Franchise owners also have to comply with the Professional Baseball Agreement, a contract that establishes relationships between the big-league clubs and their affiliates. One provision stipulates that a percentage of a minor league affiliate's ticket sales, concessions, and souvenirs goes to the parent club.

Independent teams, on the other hand, have no formal financial ties with major league baseball. Unlike franchise owners, independent team owners are responsible for their players' salaries and all other expenses, and so they may risk much more than franchise owners.

Nevertheless, most independent club owners like to be in control of their own financial destinies, and they can and have made money. According to the business magazine *Inc.*, five of the six clubs in the Northern

League showed a profit in 1993, their first year of operation. And teams under one ownership in the Texas-Louisiana League brought in revenues of $4.5 million for the 1994 season.

Whether franchise or independent, a team has to make a profit if it's going to stay in business, and a major portion of earnings comes from general admission ticket sales, including income from skyboxes that rent for $75 to $100 a night. Sometimes skyboxes are rented to corporations for an entire season, guaranteeing thousands of dollars in revenue.

Other income stems from advertising and promotion. Advertisers pay for the space they use for billboards on fences and walls around the playing field. Ads for local businesses ranging from auto repair shops to steak houses appear in team programs and other printed materials, providing additional revenue for a ballclub.

Yet teams can and do go broke. The Class A Waterloo (Iowa) Diamonds, an affiliate of the San Diego Padres, is a classic example. After years of minor league play in the Midwest League, the Diamonds lost their

CELEBRITY OWNERS

The Memphis Chicks, an affiliate of the San Diego Padres, play in McCarver Stadium, named for former big-league player and current announcer Tim McCarver, who once played for the Chicks, batting .347. McCarver is now one of the team owners. Among his partners are celebrities Ron Howard, Bob Costas, and Maury Povich.

The Kane County Cougars logo is displayed in lights on the scoreboard at their Geneva, Illinois, ballfield. Like many minor league ballparks, this one also includes a lot of billboard advertising on fences surrounding the field.

WHADDAYA KNOW...?

An avid baseball fan, Ray Nemec of Naperville, Illinois, has been compiling minor league statistics for more than fifty years and has organized data for more than 100,000 minor leaguers dating from 1870.

franchise in 1994 because of poor attendance and the town's deteriorating economic base.

Richard Panek, whose book about the Waterloo Diamonds was published in 1995, noted that Waterloo, like many other nineteenth-century cities and towns in the United States, staked its future "on manufacturing and industry, and one way they had to promote themselves was through professional baseball. If you could support a baseball team, then you were economically stable and worthy of investment. It was a way to publicize the community," Panek explained.[1] But one of Waterloo's key industries, a major packinghouse, closed, and John Deere, a large manufacturer of farming equipment, cut back its labor force. By the early 1990s, the owners of the Diamonds could no longer afford to support their team or to bring their ballpark up to the standards required by the San Diego Padres. The Diamonds' franchise went to Springfield, Illinois, in 1994. In 1996 it again shifted, going to Lansing, Michigan, where the team is known as the Lansing Lugnuts, symbolizing the city's ties with the auto industry (a name, by the way, that many fans deride).

MARKETING THE TEAMS

Bringing in fans to help spur a team on to a winning season is one of the primary mechanisms for a successful minor league operation. That process starts even before a team is in place, as has been the case with the new Lugnuts. During the summer of 1995, Lansing city officials encouraged the public to come to the site where the new minor league stadium was being built. Bleachers were put up for spectators to observe the construction. Officials said they wanted the stadium (and of course the team) to be part of the community, so it was important for citizens to participate in the stadium from the ground up.

Community participation is an important part of Leanne Harvey's marketing strategy. Harvey is one of just a few women who are general managers for minor league teams. She was hired in 1995 by the Class AAA New Orleans Zephyrs, who played their 1996 opener in a new 10,000-seat stadium. While with Class A teams Harvey became known for the techniques she used to attract fans to the ballpark even during a losing season, and in 1993 she was named one of the "Ten Most Significant Women in Baseball." Harvey told a staff reporter for the *Times Picayune* that her basic rules are to make sure the park is clean, that there is music, that flags and banners fly, and that it is "really one of the social places to be." She also insists on:

> . . . a family atmosphere . . . that's inexpensive. It's fun, wholesome entertainment . . . . The bottom line, though, is getting out in the commu-

nity and letting everybody know you're out there doing everything to get people out to the ballpark once. Usually, if you can create that atmosphere and create that fun, excitement in a Disneyland-type environment...if you get somebody out there once, they're going to come back again. [2]

Clubs use all kinds of promotions to prompt people to come to the park and entice them to continue to attend games throughout each season. When a team first forms, owners may hold a contest to name it. In 1991 the public submitted 35,000 ideas to name the Ottawa (Canada) Lynx, affiliate of the Montreal Expos and part of the

NAME THAT TEAM

Stephen McCann, an eleven-year-old baseball fan in New Hampshire, was the winner of a contest to name a new independent Class A minor league team, the Nashua Riverhawks, which opened its first season in 1995 as part of the North Atlantic Baseball League. McCann's winning name was selected from more than 500 entries, including such submissions as Nashua River Rats, Grizzlies, Salmon, Muskrats, and River Flies. The team management decided on Riverhawks because the Nashua and the Merrimack Rivers flow through the city and the name not only fit but also suggested possibilities for a logo, an important part of advertising and marketing a team. What was McCann's prize? Season tickets for the Riverhawks' games.

Triple-A International League. Lynx was chosen because the spelling is the same in English and French—both languages are native to this part of Canada. In addition, the lynx was the type of animal that suggested numerous possibilities for a logo and promotional materials.

Certainly during a holiday like the Fourth of July, club promotions at many parks include a fireworks display. At other times, there might be a laser show, or a theme weekend, such as country western or magic kingdom. Fans might be given a funny nose-and-glasses mask to wear during the game just for laughs. Perhaps one of the team members will play the national anthem on the violin—that is, if he is an accomplished violinist like pitcher Ron Frazier of the Prince William Cannons in Virginia.

One successful promotion for the Giants' Class AAA Firebirds was a "Honeymoon in Vegas Night." A lucky couple was chosen for a marriage ceremony on the ballfield and then sent on an all-expenses-paid honeymoon in Las Vegas.

At some parks, there's a promotion every time the team plays a home game. One evening there might be an Elvis Presley impersonator decked out in a sequined white suit. Another time a musical act might entertain. Or a magician might perform. Or there might be a special appearance of the Famous Chicken, an entertainer in a chicken costume who "hatched" during the 1970s in San Diego and has traveled baseball circuits ever since to perform for fans.

One very popular attraction for many years has been the Clown Prince of Baseball, Max Patkin, who once was a pitcher with the Class D Wisconsin State League.

During World War II, Patkin joined the navy and attended exhibition games for servicemen. While one game was under way, superstar Joe DiMaggio hit a home run. As DiMaggio ran the bases, Patkin followed, mimicking DiMaggio's mannerisms to the delight of the crowd. That seemed to spark his comedy career.

Patkin did his first comedy routine for pay in 1946 and since then, wearing his trademark baseball hat askew, he has performed thousands of times in minor league parks, entertaining baseball crowds with slapstick. A standard part of his routine is mugging and mimicking players, going through contortions with his long rubbery neck and gangling arms and legs.

Along with special entertainment, "freebies" are common, such as a free pizza for anyone who cheers the loudest or a gift certificate for the person who wins a footrace with the mascot or finds a lucky number in a program. The first 500 kids to enter the ballpark may win a lunch box, baseball, floppy hat, T-shirt, mini bat, or some other prize. Or the person with the dirtiest car in the parking lot may be given a certificate for a free car wash. During the 1994 and 1995 seasons, the South Bend (Indiana) Silver Hawks, with the cooperation of a local jeweler, gave away a free watch worth $100 to

WHADDAYA KNOW...?

A regulation baseball bat is made of solid wood, usually ash, and is no more than 42 inches (106.68 centimeters) long.

$125 during each home game, picking a fan at random for the gift. When the Pittsfield Mets were playing the Batavia Clippers, they held a Clip the Clippers Night—barbers gave free haircuts to fans. A top promotion for the Frederick (Maryland) Keys was a series of give-aways. Every Tuesday night for five weeks, youngsters attending the game received one part of a baseball out-fit. By the end of the five weeks a fan could collect a baseball helmet, bat, glove, ball, and jersey.

A frequently used method for promoting a minor league team is to offer group sales at special rates, as low as a few dollars per person. Rates are based on the size of the groups, which can range from ten or twelve for a kid's birthday celebration, to several hundred for a family reunion, to more than a thousand for a company picnic. Usually the group package includes reserved seating, a picnic lunch or simple refreshments such as hot dogs, peanuts, and soft drinks, and some type of souvenir.

CONCESSION AND SOUVENIR STANDS

Concession and souvenir sales can bring in several hun-dred thousand dollars per year for a minor league club. But beyond the profits, every owner or manager knows that certain foods are part of the ballgame: popcorn, peanuts, caramel corn, burritos, nachos, hamburgers, pizza, french fries, barbecued ribs, candy apples, sno-cones, funnel cakes, cotton candy...the list goes on. And who can watch baseball without eating a hot dog? The

The concession stand brings in revenue for a baseball club. Foods like hot dogs, hamburgers, pizza, and popcorn are favorites with fans.

two activities go together. In fact, at least 9 percent of the hot dogs consumed in the United States are eaten in baseball parks.

The very name for the hot dog came from its legendary association with baseball. As the story goes, sausages in buns were first sold at baseball games in 1900 and were called dachshunds because their shape called to mind the low-slung body of the dog by that name. Vendors often called out "Red hot dachshund! Get your hot dachshund sausage!" Then one day, a cartoon published in a New York newspaper showed a vendor selling a barking sandwich, and since the illustrator, cartoonist Tad Dorgan, couldn't spell "dachshund," he used

SPECIALTY FOODS

While the food served at baseball parks certainly is not gourmet, some minor league ballparks are known for their mouth-watering specialties. The Firedog, a spicy hot dog served at Bush Stadium in Indianapolis for years, will probably continue to be served when the Indianapolis Indians move into a new downtown facility in 1996. Barbecued ribs have been called "memorable" at the Durham Bulls park in Durham, North Carolina. A favorite at Grant Field, home of the Dunedin Blue Jays, an affiliate of the Toronto Blue Jays, is a grilled back bacon sandwich. At the Zephyrs' park in New Orleans, the Muffaletta, an Italian bread sandwich made with salami, cheese, and olive spread, is a specialty.

the term "hot dog." Ever since then vendors have sold "hot dogs" or "red hots!"

National advertising often spurs sales of concession items such as sports drinks, sodas, and beer at ballgames. When Michael Jordan played with the Birmingham Barons, he was shown in TV commercials for Gatorade, pitching the drink by saying "When I played basketball, I always wanted the ball. And I got it where it should go. And I always drank Gatorade, 'cause nothing's better. Now I'm playing baseball. I still drink Gatorade, I still want the ball. And I still know where it should go. And sooner or later, I'm gonna get it there." But he didn't. Jordan left baseball, and the commercial is now a thing of the past.

Souvenirs are almost guaranteed moneymakers at most ballparks. Topping the list of favored products are, of course, baseball caps, T-shirts, and sweatshirts with trademarked team logos that range from a baseball peeping from the top of a corn stalk (representing the Cedar Rapids Kernels of Iowa) to a snorting bull (the symbol of the Durham Bulls). Mini bats and mitts, mugs, pennants, pencils, pens, stuffed animals, lunch boxes, and dozens of other items are offered for sale to bring in revenue for a club. A popular souvenir item is the official program booklet that may contain a page of collectible baseball cards, perforated for easy removal, and "twofer" coupons offering two general admissions for the price of one ticket.

ECONOMIC IMPACT

Clubs do their best to make a profit, but they also have an economic impact—usually beneficial—on the local community. One of the most obvious is summer jobs. For the most part, local people are hired to take tickets, work at concession and souvenir stands, maintain the park, usher, operate sound and lighting equipment, and handle publicity and public relations. Local vendors— ice cream, pizza, and hot dog suppliers, breweries, soft drink companies, and other wholesalers—sell products to the park. A minor league club is also involved in fundraising efforts for civic projects and local charity programs.

It is common for cities and towns to receive some of the receipts from games, if the community has provided the park or stadium, which is often the case even in Rookie ball. Bluefield, West Virginia, for example, hosts the Bluefield Orioles, the Appalachian League's Rookie team affiliated with the major club in Baltimore. The town government paid for the construction of Bowen Field ballpark and maintains it, and in compensation the Baltimore Orioles club turns over the income from ticket sales to Bluefield.

In larger communities, local and county governments have issued bonds to help raise money for a new ballpark or sports complex, which provides construction work for local people and eventually brings in revenue. Total costs for a new structure can be $8 million to $10 million or more. To pay off the bonds and maintain the facilities, a local government collects sales tax, rent, or a portion of a team's profits.

The new Durham Bulls stadium in North Carolina, with a seating capacity of almost 10,000, reportedly cost $16.1 million, and funds for the project were raised through local taxes. A series of news releases from the Bulls throughout 1994 and early 1995 kept the public informed about the progress of construction, which helped build interest and maintain private and public support for the club.

The local media and curious Bulls fans gathered periodically to watch some of the final stages of the Durham park construction, such as laying the sod to cover the infield, outfield, and foul territory. Using strips 50 to 60 feet (15 to 18 meters) long, 4 feet (1.2 meters) wide, and 2 inches (5 centimeters) thick, it took the better part of a week for groundskeepers to cover the total

Bill Larsen, general manager of the Kane County Cougars, checks out activities in the stadium and on the field via a two-way radio.

2.5 acres (1 hectare). Below the playing surface is a state-of-the art drainage system that allows rain to run off quickly and helps to ensure that a game begins on time or continues after a sudden downpour.

In Illinois, the Kane County Forest Preserve District owns the park where the Class A Cougars play. For several years the district leased the facility to the team owners and received 10 percent of the profits. Because the Cougars have been highly successful, bringing in an average of 6,800 fans during home games, the club owners asked the district to expand and renovate the ballpark.

Negotiations between club owners and local officials are an ongoing process in many parts of North America as minor leagues try to improve their clubs, facilities, and entertainment appeal. In early 1995, Don Beaver, who owns three teams, began talks with Winston-Salem, North Carolina, officials to renovate Ernie Shore Stadium, where one of his teams plays. He wants to add skyboxes, a press box, and additional seating to help draw crowds. To spark interest, he also renamed the team the Warthogs (it was formerly known as the

WHADDAYA KNOW...?

In spite of harassment, low pay, and lack of support for her goal to reach the majors, Pam Postema worked as a minor league umpire for thirteen years, from 1977 through 1989, the longest period that any woman has held a field position in a major professional sport.

Winston-Salem Spirits). The name provides more opportunities for developing promotional materials and events.

When negotiating to buy a team, Beaver points to his success with the Hickory Crawdads of the South Atlantic League. In his first year of ownership, Beaver reported that the Crawdads brought in about $1 million in ticket sales and $700,000 in concession sales. The city receives twenty-five cents on each ticket and 10 percent of all concessions sales as repayment for the $2 million the city provided to build the Crawdads' stadium. Reportedly, the city revenues from the Crawdads totaled more than $178,000 in 1993 and more than $184,000 in 1994.

The secret of success for any minor league ballpark, as with any other business, lies with the customers. If they don't come to the games, everyone loses. So most general managers and front-office personnel work very hard to ensure that minor league baseball is a community affair.

6 A COMMUNITY AFFAIR

"Take me out to the ballgame . . . !" It's a familiar re-frain. And going to a nearby park to "root, root, root for the home team" seems especially significant to many minor league fans who definitely have a proprietary feel-ing about their hometown club. Some have personal relationships with minor league players, particularly if players stay with local families or are invited to dinners at various homes. Players may also attend parties with residents or take part in other civic events that foster friendships.

Going to the ballpark to root for a player you know personally is great. But even if you have no personal connections with the team, a friendly atmosphere would likely prevail at a typical park. Most fans enjoy the game in the company of friends or relatives. It's also a way for parents and grandparents to spend time with their kids and to get to know each other.

Certainly, many fans go to the ballpark strictly for the game—they want to watch "pure" baseball. However, some purists complain about the lack of continuity of players, managers, and coaches even though that's to be expected with farm teams; they're in the business of promoting or weeding out players. Another drawback for some is the carnival atmosphere, but the rise in attendance at minor league parks is almost always linked to marketing gimmicks. By far, most spectators seem to want the added incentives.

Whatever your reason for going to a minor league game, chances are you'll be infected sooner or later by the festive mood. So put on your lucky hat, jacket, shoes, or T-shirt and sing the rest of the song as you head for the old ballpark.

AT THE PARK

On arrival at a minor league stadium, you might see a lot of activity in the parking lot. Maybe some folks are playing Frisbee. Others may be having a tailgate party or, depending on the location, getting ready to watch the game from a hot tub in the park or even from one installed in the back of a pickup truck! Perhaps, as was the case in a Midwest park, some young fans will be shooting baskets through a mounted hoop on the back of a van while they wait for the baseball game to begin. In short, the community gathers for an entertaining and recreational evening.

Since most minor league games are at night, the lights illuminate not only the field and stands but also the area around the park. Music is probably blasting from the loudspeakers. The smell of popcorn or hot dogs may tempt you, and you may need a soda to wash down your snack. Maybe you'll want to see how fast you can throw a baseball in a test cage where a radar gun monitors your speed.

If you are an autograph collector, you can usually get players to sign your program or souvenir baseball or whatever. You can line up with other autograph seekers waiting for players to finish warmups and pass by the gate to the dugout. If you've brought your camera, there could be an opportunity for snapping a picture of your favorite player.

As you find your seat in the stands, diamond girls—glorified cheerleaders in some type of uniform—may be performing their act. The team mascot is probably on hand, distributing giveaways and greeting fans in humorous mime. Mascots are a part of the entertainment, and some spectators would insist that these professional clowns in costume are as important to the game as the players.

WHADDAYA KNOW...?

With the aid of video cameras, researchers have found that even though a fly ball may appear to travel in a straight line, fielders do not run along a straight path. Rather they travel at varying speeds and change directions in order to catch the ball.

HOMEGROWN TEAM MASCOTS

A mascot is a must for a minor league team. It might be a trained pig, like the one used by the Saint Paul (Minnesota) Saints to carry balls to the home plate umpire whenever the supply is low. The Durham Bulls once had a live bull as a mascot, and other four-legged creatures have occasionally been paraded as a team's good-luck symbol.

When a new mascot joins a club, a contest is usually held to name him, her, or it. More than 500 entries were submitted in 1992 to name the Bulls' new Wool E. Bull, now played by an actor in costume. His first birthday was celebrated by the club in 1993 with hundreds of kids attending the party. It's all part of the club and community promotion effort.

The role of a team mascot is usually played by a local person, someone who lives and works in the area where the hometown team plays. Ron Metz of Kane County plays the role of Ozzie for the Class A Cougars and also doubles as a groundskeeper at Elfstrom Stadium just outside Geneva, Illinois, where the Cougars play.

In the Toledo, Ohio, area, Steve Sophis is employed as a supermarket manager, but also works part time as Muddy the Mud Hen, named for the Toledo Mud Hens, a Class AAA affiliate of the Detroit Tigers. The name of the team probably originated around 1895 when games were played in a park surrounded by marshes where wild ducks and ducklike birds called mudhens found refuge. Since the birds flew about frequently, the name Mud Hens seemed a natural for the team and the mascot, who came along much later.

"Muddy the Mud Hen," mascot for the Toledo Mud hens, cavorts for fans.

Today, Muddy is costumed somewhat like the real bird. His garb includes a huge mask with a beak, yellow tights, and a pair of high-top shoes—the popular Converse brand. In 1993, Muddy signed a contract with the footwear company to promote their product as his dancing shoes. Part of his routine is to boogie with a volunteer atop the dugout roof.

Sophis has been a hit with fans since his first season in 1990, and he's credited with helping to increase attendance at the park, which is located at the Lucas County Recreation Center just southwest of Toledo in suburban Maumee. Before the ballgame, he greets people with the pounding of his bat—his "speaking" voice. He's in charge of giveaway drawings and contests, such as home-run hitting and racing against young fans along the basepath. During the footrace, he manages to trip or "do something stupid" as a crowd pleaser and to ensure that a youngster will win. He provides the kind of entertainment that fans appreciate. In the words of the Mud Hens' media-relations director: "His popularity in the area is tremendous. He does such a great job. We get him out to all kinds of parades, hospitals to visit kids and charity functions." As for Sophis, the role he plays is "a release from the normal world . . . you can [act] crazy, and nobody knows you, or you don't care what anybody thinks."[1] In short, he loves performing.

Like Muddy the Mud Hen, other local mascots have been popular with their fans. One is Covey, who represents Hall of Fame major league pitcher Stanley Coveleski, namesake of Stanley Coveleski Regional Stadium in South Bend, Indiana, where the Silver Hawks play. Then there's Tremor, the "Rallysaurus," mascot

Covey, the mascot for the South Bend, Indiana, Silver Hawks, hands a baseball to a young fan who will throw out the first pitch of the season.

for the Class A Quakes, who often brings fans to their feet as they cheer for his dancing at the Epicenter, the stadium in Rancho Cucamonga, California. In South Carolina, Homer the Green Dragon is a popular mascot who has led hundreds of kids around Knights Castle, as it's nicknamed, the ballpark that is home for the Charlotte Knights, a Triple-A affiliate of the Florida Marlins.

Bird mascots from the New Haven Ravens and the New Jersey Cardinals and a raccoon from the Hudson Valley Renegades prance around minor league parks within 75 miles (120 kilometers) of metropolitan New York City. In other areas, you can find a mascot that resembles a blue jay, redbird, or hawk; a bison, fox, polecat, or tiger; a wizard, Canadian mounty, duke, or pirate.

Ozzie Cougar, mascot for the Kane County Cougers, poses for fans before the game begins.

Some teams have an assistant mascot, too, such as a Mr. Trash who cavorts about the park picking up waste paper and other debris. The mascot not only saves the club cleanup expenses, but promotes environmentally sound habits as well!

MINOR LEAGUE BOOSTERS

Members of booster clubs, as their name implies, plan and conduct numerous kinds of programs to boost their team. Perhaps they sponsor a kids club to get youngsters involved with baseball. Or a club might publicize road trips to make the circuit for league games, providing a map of team locations and a list of accommodations nearby.

Suppose you're in Raleigh, North Carolina. A half-hour drive takes you to either the Durham Bulls or the Carolina Mudcats. In Kinston there's a Carolina League farm team, and at Fayetteville the Detroit Tigers' farm team plays. A Rookie League for the Cleveland Indians is in Burlington, and the Bats, a New York Yankee affiliate, play A ball in Greensboro. Just off Interstate 40 are the Winston-Salem Warthogs, the Hickory Crawdads, and the Asheville Tourists. The Charlotte Knights, a step below a major league team, can be found at Fort Mill.

WHADDAYA KNOW...?

Syndicated columnist George Will was named commissioner of the Texas-Louisiana League in 1995.

Out West, some folks plan a camping vacation around Pacific Coast League teams, traveling to and through Vancouver, British Columbia; Calgary and Edmonton in Alberta, Canada; Tacoma, Washington; Salt Lake City, Utah; Colorado Springs, Colorado; Las Vegas, Nevada; Albuquerque, New Mexico; and Phoenix and Tucson, Arizona (not necessarily in that order). People who combine their love of baseball with their enthusiasm for camping often get to enjoy spectacular sights as well, from glacier vistas in Canada to views of Pikes Peak in Colorado.

Minor league boosters (along with paid promoters) also tout such attractions as the Great Wall of Cheney in Tacoma's Cheney Stadium. Because of the winds in Tacoma, no player has ever been able to hit a home run over its 32-foot center-field wall during a game. However, in 1985, while Jose Canseco (now with the Boston Red Sox) was still in the minors, he hit one over the top during batting practice.

Wherever there are loyal minor league fans, there are folks who have nostalgic ties to their team and the stadium where their games are played. In Eugene, Oregon, for example, townsfolks view their stadium as part of their personal history. It was built in 1938 by workers in the Works Progress Administration program, better known as the WPA, set up to provide jobs for the masses of unemployed during the Great Depression. Anyone who watches from the grandstand sits on gray, backless benches made of two planks laid side by side with some 5,600 places marked off, although another 1,000 modern box seats were added a few years ago. "This is a nice place to spend a summer evening in Oregon," one

FROM KAZOOS TO CATS

The Battle Creek Golden Kazoos dropped their team name before they even played a game during the 1995 season. Many fans in Battle Creek and Kalamazoo, Michigan, were unhappy with the moniker, and rumor has it that one disgruntled individual learned that the name had never been legally registered. So he decided to register the name and then offer to sell it to the team for $100,000. As expected, the team declined. They decided to call themselves the Michigan Battle Cats.

fan commented. "Class A ball is a little like high school ball. In one game, they're pretty hard to beat. In the next, they all fall apart." [2]

When a team has to move, as often happens, there is real grief. That's already been expressed by fans and boosters of the Firebirds, who have played in Scottsdale, Arizona, for several years. The Firebirds will be forced out of Scottsdale when the major league Diamondbacks make the city their home base in 1998, and fans of the minor league team feel they, too, will be pushed aside for the high-priced entertainment. Sue Toth, president of the Firebirds booster club, summed up club member attitudes in an interview with a sports reporter: "Once the majors come in...the little people [will be] just kind of lost in the shuffle. We'll be out of baseball." [3]

Just because the majors expand does not mean minor league fans necessarily lose out, however. In some parts of the United States, major and minor league teams

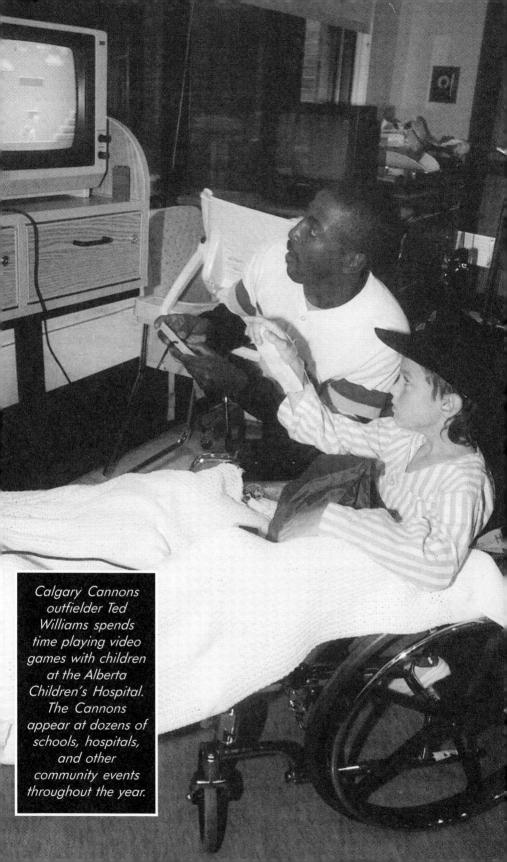

Calgary Cannons outfielder Ted Williams spends time playing video games with children at the Alberta Children's Hospital. The Cannons appear at dozens of schools, hospitals, and other community events throughout the year.

operate within a few minutes to an hour's drive of each other and both draw crowds. Such is the case in Minnesota. The successful St. Paul Saints are located about 6 miles (10 kilometers) from the Metrodome where the Minnesota Twins play. In Washington, the popular Triple-A Tacoma Rainiers play in a stadium (which offers spectators a view of Mount Rainier) that is minutes away from the Seattle Mariners. Pawtucket, Rhode Island, is less than a hour from Boston, Massachusetts, but fans still flock to see its Triple-A team, an affiliate of the Boston Red Sox. And in Akron, Ohio, city officials and residents look forward to 1997 when the Class AA Indians, an affiliate of the Cleveland (Ohio) Indians, move from Canton to Akron, which is just a short drive from Cleveland.

In the opinion of Miles Wolff, owner of *Baseball America* magazine and past owner and general manager of several teams, a new ballpark in downtown Akron "will be a magnet" that will draw people to an area needing an economic boost. "People in big-league markets crave minor league baseball" because it's "cheaper than the big leagues [and] players are more accessible. It's just a lot more fun," Wolff declared.[4]

WHADDAYA KNOW...?

A maintenance man for the Billings (Montana) Mustangs, a Pioneer League Rookie team, has been known to dry the infield with a blowtorch.

7 THE CHANGING SCENE

Clearly, changes are part of the minor league scene and the constant shifts and alterations in teams and players can be difficult to follow. By faithfully attending games, however, many fans keep track of their favorite players. They also learn about those who have been promoted by reading biographical sketches in club programs. Here, for example, is how the Albuquerque Dukes, in their 1994 season magazine, sketched part of the career of one of their players, catcher Mike Piazza, who went on to the Los Angeles Dodgers:

Duke fans saw what Piazza could do before he ever arrived in L.A. In 1992, Mike came to Albuquerque barely a month into the season after tearing up the Texas League in his 31 games with San Antonio. He batted .377 in his brief time in

Double A, hitting seven homers and driving in 20 runs [actually 21] before joining the Dukes. Triple A pitching did not slow Piazza, however, as he put together a 25-game hitting streak . . . 16 home runs and 69 RBI in just 94 games . . . .

Piazza's amazing success did not come without hard work, however. Despite the spectacular numbers he posted with San Antonio and Albuquerque in 1992, Mike entered spring training in 1993 as a long shot at best to win the starting catcher's job. After all, he was going up against veteran[s] . . . He went into spring training . . . on a mission, though, and by the end of the Grapefruit League [Florida circuit] schedule he had established himself as the Dodgers Opening Day catcher. [1]

OTHER WAYS TO TRACK THE MINORS

Minor league games may be shown on a local cable TV channel, broadcast on the radio, or reported in newspapers. The 1995 opening game between the Midwest League's West Michigan Whitecaps of Grand Rapids

Many minor league fans follow the progress of their favorite players, such as the Albuquerque Dukes' popular shortstop Rafel Bournigal, shown here at the plate.

and the South Bend (Indiana) Silver Hawks was covered by eight TV news crews as well as sportswriters from five area newspapers. Such game coverage often includes updates on players.

Another way to stay informed is to check out such publications as *USA Today Baseball Weekly, The Sporting News,* and the annual *Baseball America's Directory.* If a player becomes a star, usually an autobiography or a biography detailing his career is published in a sports magazine or in book form. Several books on the minor leagues also contain such information (see Further Reading). And don't forget individual baseball cards that show a player's record along with the minor and major league teams for which he's played.

ELECTRONIC FORUMS

One place to get the latest information on baseball, including minor league activity, is through an electronic subscription service such as America Online or CompuServe. These services offer news and a variety of forums, such as ones dedicated to ongoing discussions about baseball.

Usually, after joining a sports forum, all you have to do is type a question or comment and someone will respond. Or you can simply read information that people have posted. Those knowledgeable about the game like to share what they know—whether it's statistics on major league teams or information about minor leagues. In fact, some research information for this book came from a sports forum. One item was an article on the Arizona

BROADCASTING A GAME BY BRAILLE

One of the most unusual broadcast teams in minor league baseball calls the games of the New Britain Rock Cats, a Double-A Eastern League team in Connecticut. It is composed of two men and a dog. The men are Don Wardlow, who has been blind from birth, and his sighted partner, Jim Lucas. Gizmo, a Labrador retriever, is Wardlow's guide.

How do the three work together? Reportedly, Lucas collects the latest statistics on the team and their opponent and puts the information on a tape recorder, which Wardlow transcribes into braille. Both written and braille scorebooks are available at the ballpark. During the game Lucas broadcasts the play-by-play and Wardlow the color. Even though Wardlow has never seen a game, he bases his images on statistics, crowd reaction to the team announcer, and earlier interviews with players, spectators, and others. By the way, the team gets its own advertisers for their broadcasts; one is a dog-food company, assuring that Gizmo will eat even if the rest of the team doesn't!

Fall League, and the posting included an E-mail address to subscribe to *Diamond Alert,* a newsletter about baseball. Another posting listed the current names of minor league teams and the stadiums and towns where they play. A third described a new book, *Rebel Baseball* by Steve Perlstein, which tells how the Northern League was founded and focuses on the St. Paul (Minnesota)

Minor league players help make baseball a community affair by visiting fans who are hospitalized. Here, the Albuquerque Dukes lift the spirits of Lorenzo Oriveros at a community hospital.

WHADDAYA KNOW...?

An outfielder on the Durham Bulls team in 1995 stole nine bases in his first nine games with the team. His name is Wonderful Monds.

Saints, run by Mike Veeck, son of the legendary Bill Veeck, Jr.

Sometimes participants want answers to specific questions, such as this inquiry sent out by a ninth grader:

I am doing a project for school on the issue: "Is baseball a business?" I was planning on a good part of my information coming from you guys: the baseball fans on [CompuServe]. Any comments at all you might have on the issue would be helpful . . . .

Please take 5 minutes to fill this thing out and write back with any suggestions, ideas, or info that would be helpful. Remember: You are the fans, ultimately what you say counts. I'll try to post the results on the forum when my project is finished . . . .

The questionnaire followed, and the ninth grader ended his message with his own opinion about the business of baseball: "I'd rather go watch a minor league game with low ticket prices because it's more fun. A night at a MLB [major league baseball] park costs way too much."

Many people agree with that assessment. But beyond the low price and fun experienced at minor league games, fans across the continent seem to be saying their teams are really not "minor" in the sense of their popularity and the way they represent the true spirit of baseball. Fans clearly like to root for their home team and watch 'em play ball—win or lose.

NOTES

CHAPTER 1
FROM BANDITS TO POLECATS!

1. Quoted in Robert Fachet, "On a Minor Scale, Promotions Are the Key to True Harmony," *The Washington Post,* June 29, 1993, Sports section.
2. Quoted in Bob Verdi, "Sandberg Enjoys Refresher Course," *Chicago Tribune,* May 4, 1993, Sports section.
3. Quoted in Gary Horowitz, "Firebirds Won at the Gate," *The Arizona Republic,* September 7, 1994.
4. J. A. Leatherman, "Replace Major Leagues, Bring Baseball to Home Towns," *The Elkhart Truth,* March 28, 1995, People's Forum section.
5. Quoted in David Garth, "Green Running Out of Chances for Major League Career," *Pittsburgh Post-Gazette,* June 1, 1995.
6. Quoted in Jack Curry, "The Replacements: Lost in the Shuffle," *Charlotte Observer,* April 3, 1995.

CHAPTER 3
TODAY'S MINOR LEAGUES

1. George F. Will, *Men at Work: The Craft of Baseball* (New York: Harper Perennial, HarperCollins, 1990), p. 187.

2. Quoted in Alan Moyer, "A New Idea for the Major Leagues," *Arizona Fall League 1992 Inaugural Program,* p. 2.
3. R. J. Harrison, "Scouts Honor," *AVIS Arizona Fall League 1994 Season Program,* p. 71.
4. Quoted in Jeff Babineau, "On the Mend," *Orlando Sentinel,* July 31, 1994.
5. Quoted in Ric Russo, "This Old Man Keeps Career Afloat Amidst Sea of Youth," *Orlando Sentinel,* July 25, 1993.
6. Steve Fireovid and Mark Winegardner, *The 26th Man: One Minor League Pitcher's Pursuit of a Dream* (New York: Macmillan, 1991), p. 5.

CHAPTER 4
FROM "BUS LEAGUES"
TO THE MAJORS
1. Quoted in Ken Wheeler, "A for Effort," *Oregonian,* July 24, 1994.
2. Quoted in Paul Sullivan, "Still Laid-Back, Radinsky Back," *Chicago Tribune,* April 9, 1995, Sports section.

CHAPTER 5
THE BUSINESS SIDE
OF THE GAMES
1. Quoted in John Blades, "America's Past Time," *Chicago Tribune,* August 7, 1995, Tempo section.
2. Quoted in Peter Barrouquere, "Z'S GM Has Plans to Create Family Atmosphere," *New Orleans Times Picayune,* April 2, 1995, Sports section.

CHAPTER 6
A COMMUNITY AFFAIR
1. Quoted in Jason Butler, "A Hen Who Never Lays an Egg," *Akron Beacon Journal,* August 28, 1994.
2. Quoted in Ken Wheeler, "A for Effort," *Oregonian,* July 24, 1994.
3. Quoted in Deron Snyder, "With Expansion, Squeeze Play Is on for Firebirds," *USA Today Baseball Weekly,* April 12-18, 1995.

4. Quoted in Terry Pluto, "Expert on Minors Likes Area's Prospect," *Akron Beacon Journal,* July 16, 1995, Sports section.

CHAPTER 7
THE CHANGING SCENE

1. "Piazza Has a Season for the Ages," *Dukes 1994 Season Magazine*, p. 82.

FURTHER
READING

Adelson, Bruce, Rod Beaton, Bill Koenig, and Lisa Winston. *The Minor League Baseball Book.* New York: Macmillan Travel, 1995.

Allen, Glen. "The Capital Gang, Ottawa Fans Embrace Minor-League Baseball," *Macleans*, August 9, 1993, p. 48.

Blahnik, Judith, and Phillip Stephen Schulz. *Mud Hens and Mavericks.* New York: Viking Studio Books, 1995.

Bosco, Joseph. *The Boys Who Would Be Cubs: A Year in the Heart of Baseball's Minor Leagues.* New York: William Morrow, 1990.

Dolson, Frank. *Beating the Bushes.* South Bend, IN: Icarus Press, 1982.

Elliott, Lawrence. "Field of Dreams," *Reader's Digest*, June 1994, pp. 47-51.

Fireovid, Steve, and Mark Winegardner. *The 26th Man: One Minor League Pitcher's Pursuit of a Dream.* New York: Macmillan, 1991.

Helmer, Diana Star. *Belles of the Ballpark.* Brookfield, CT: Millbrook Press, 1993.

Johnson, Lloyd, and Miles Wolff, eds. *The Encyclopedia of Minor League Baseball.* Durham, NC: Baseball America, 1993.

Johnson, Susan E. *When Women Played Hardball.* Seattle, WA: Seal Press, 1994.

Lamb, David. *Stolen Season: A Journey Through America and Baseball's Minor Leagues.* New York: Random House, 1991.

Margolies, Jacob. *The Negro Leagues: The Story of Black Baseball.* New York: Franklin Watts, 1993.

Obojski, Robert. *Bush League: A History of Minor League Baseball.* New York: Macmillan, 1975.

Panek, Richard. *Waterloo Diamonds.* New York: St. Martin's Press, 1995.

Perlstein, Steve. *Rebel Baseball: The Summer the Game Was Returned to the Fans.* New York: Holt, 1995.

Postema, Pam, and Gene Wojciechowski. *You've Got to Have Balls to Make It in This League: My Life as an Umpire.* New York: Simon & Schuster, 1992.

Schiffres, Manuel. "Buying Into Baseball," *Kiplinger's Personal Finance Magazine*, October 1992, pp. 72-76.

Simpson, Alan, ed. *Baseball America's 1995 Directory: The Complete Pocket Baseball Guide.* Durham, NC: Baseball America, 1995.

"The Minors Go Big," *The Economist*, July 23, 1994, p. 87.

Ward, Geoffrey C., and Ken Burns. *Baseball: An Illustrated History*. New York: Alfred A. Knopf, 1994.

Whitford, David. "Diamonds in the Rough," *Inc.*, November 1994, pp. 82-92.

Will, George E. *Men At Work: The Craft of Baseball*. New York: Harper Perennial, HarperCollins, 1990.

Witteman, Paul A. "The Only Game in Town," *Time*, August 22, 1994, pp. 76-77.

INDEX